Born
in the
Wild

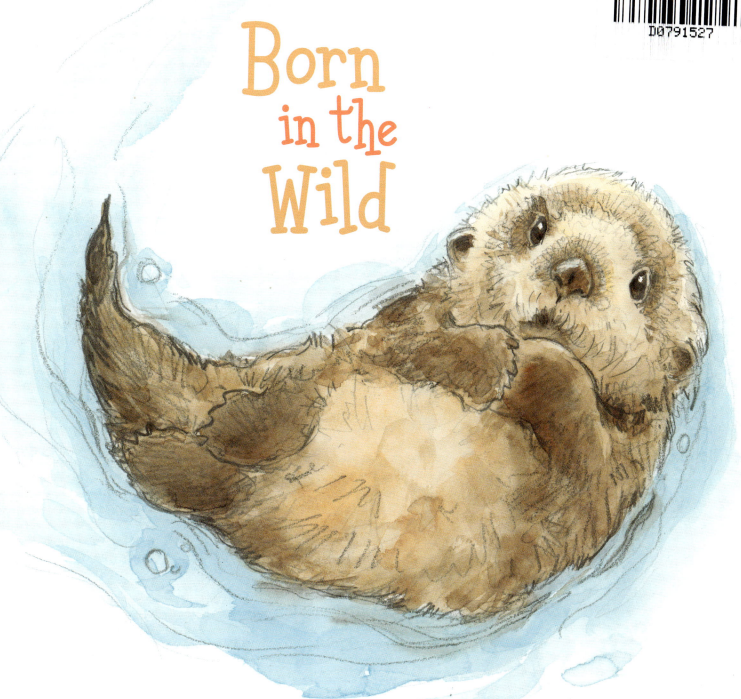

Born in the Wild

Baby Mammals and Their Parents

Lita Judge

SCHOLASTIC INC.

A baby is born.

Polar bear cubs arrive tiny, blind, and nearly hairless. They may grow to weigh over 900 pounds, but at birth they are no bigger than squirrels. The cubs sleep and stay warm against their mother's fur. In a few months they'll be big enough to explore the world outside their den.

Other babies look like little adults and are ready to run!
A giraffe calf is born in open country where lions prowl.
After some shaky stumbles, she wobbles to her feet. Within
hours she may need to sprint from danger.

The baby is hungry!

All mammals begin life nursing on their mother's milk.

Grizzly bear cubs nurse for several months before they start eating grasses, berries, insects, and a little meat. But they won't be weaned from their mother's rich milk for two or three years.

Wolf pups grow tiny teeth in their first three weeks. But meat is tough so the pups rely on adults chewing and regurgitating it. Within two months the pups will have adult teeth and can eat meat brought back to the den.

A two-week-old guanaco calf begins to eat a little grass. Over the next few months she will depend less and less on her mother's milk, until she is weaned entirely.

The baby needs protection.

Mammals are born small and defenseless—they need to be kept safe from danger.

In his first few days, a white-tailed deer fawn is too wobbly and frail to run, so he hides by staying perfectly still. His mother comes back to nurse him occasionally, but most of the time she stays away so hungry predators don't find him.

A mother panda protects her cub by cradling him to her chest. For several days after he is born, she won't even put him down to eat or drink. It will be months before he is strong enough to support his own weight. Until then, he depends on his mother to hold him safe.

A musk ox calf is strong enough to endure harsh Arctic storms, but she is defenseless against hungry wolves. With sharp horns, snorts, and stamps, the entire herd forms a tight, protective circle around the little one, guarding against attacks.

The baby needs shelter.

Animals need to be protected from rain, wind, and snow, and shaded from hot sun.

Young western harvest mice, called pinkies, grow quickly in nests their mothers weave with grass and downy plants.

Badger cubs stay sheltered with their mother in the burrow she digs underground.

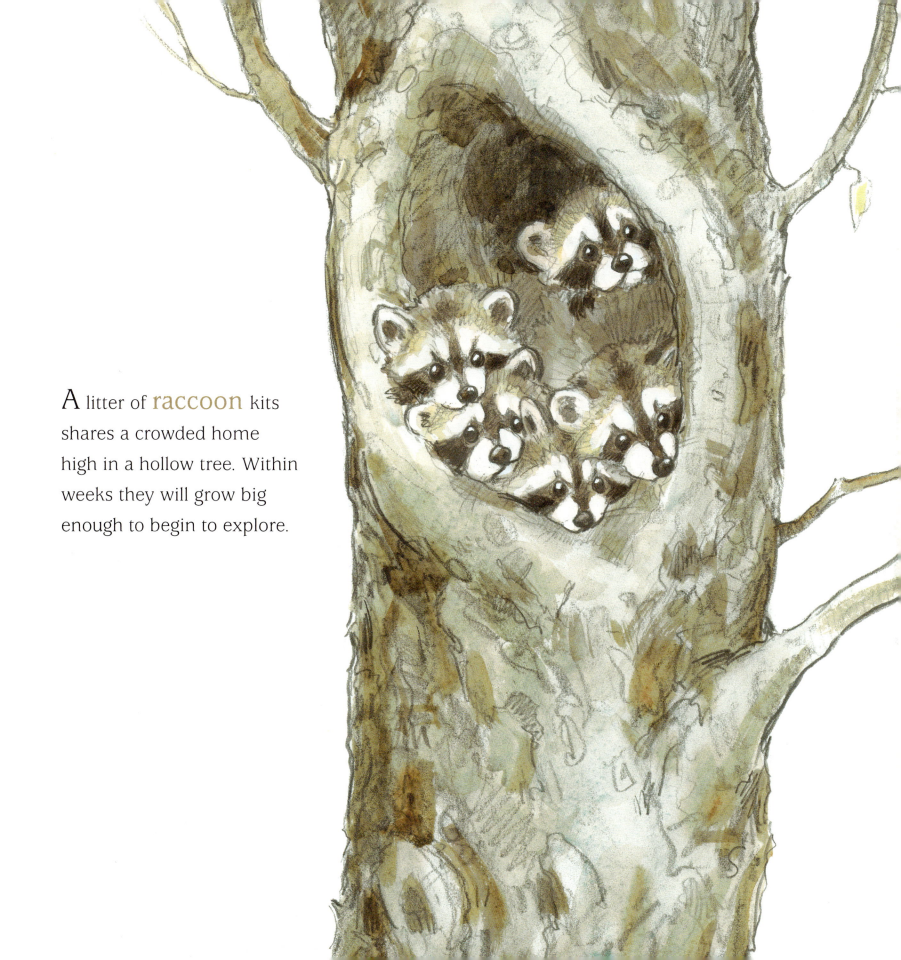

A litter of raccoon kits shares a crowded home high in a hollow tree. Within weeks they will grow big enough to begin to explore.

The baby needs to move.

A newborn mammal might need to keep up with its mother as she searches for food or flees from danger.

Eastern gray kangaroos are marsupials. The baby, called a joey, is protected and carried by his mother in a special pouch. Wherever she goes, he goes too.

Virginia opossums are also marsupials. But there are so many joeys in this family they soon outgrow their mother's pouch. They cling to her back while she roams about. Hold on tight!

A plains zebra colt is born with long, wobbly legs that soon grow strong. Within hours he can leap and run from predators that stalk his herd.

The baby is part of a family.

Animal families can
be large or small.

A mother hippopotamus gives birth to a single calf. Soon
after birth the pair joins other females and their babies. Their
group is called a school, and together the mothers protect the
calves from lions and other predators.

Red fox kits grow up with several siblings. A mother fox usually has a litter of four to six kits, sometimes more. The father fox brings food back to the den and helps protect them.

Only two to four pups join a meerkat family, called a mob, each year. Parents, older siblings, cousins, aunts, and uncles all protect and teach them.

The baby needs to be caressed and groomed.

To grow healthy, newborns need stimulation and attention.

Baby cougars cuddle close to their mother. She grooms her cubs tenderly and sleeps curled around them, keeping them safe and warm.

A chimpanzee infant is inseparable from her mother. But other female chimps and their youngsters also form strong bonds with the new baby, touching, holding hands, and playing with the little one. This nurturing will ensure she becomes a successful member of their community.

A newborn elephant calf gets lots of reassurance from her mother, aunts, and grandmothers. The family welcomes the calf by touching her with their trunks, as if to say, "Are you okay?"

The baby grows strong through play.

Youngsters build grown-up skills by jumping, chasing, and roughhousing.

Ring-tailed lemur infants are curious and eager to explore. They hop as if their legs were made of springs. Soon they'll be nimble enough to leap through the trees.

Stalk, run, quick attack! **Lion** parents are tolerant of their cubs' games of hunt and chase. The cubs will need these skills to survive.

Pushing and shoving, mountain goat kids play "King of the Rock." This may be fun, but mock battles also prepare young male billies to compete for mates when they become adults.

The baby learns.

Young mammals must be taught to find food and be alert for danger if they are to survive to adulthood.

"*Chirr—erp!*" A mother pika screams an alarm as a hawk flies overhead. Her youngsters learn that hawks are dangerous. They race back to their den.

Before he can swim, a sea otter pup watches his mother. She teaches him to swim and dive, to find clams and urchins for food, and to crack open tough shells with a rock.

It takes a young orangutan at least ten years to discover all he needs to know. As he grows up his mother shows him where to find food, how to do more complicated things, like using sticks for tools, and even how to build a sleeping nest of leafy branches in the trees.

Kits and joeys, cubs and colts—
every baby mammal needs gentle
care and teaching . . .

just like you!

More about the animals in this book

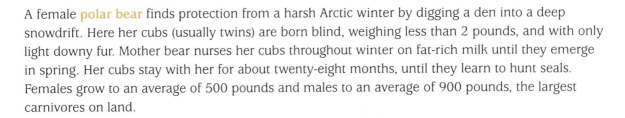

A female **polar bear** finds protection from a harsh Arctic winter by digging a den into a deep snowdrift. Here her cubs (usually twins) are born blind, weighing less than 2 pounds, and with only light downy fur. Mother bear nurses her cubs throughout winter on fat-rich milk until they emerge in spring. Her cubs stay with her for about twenty-eight months, until they learn to hunt seals. Females grow to an average of 500 pounds and males to an average of 900 pounds, the largest carnivores on land.

A baby **reticulated giraffe** has a shocking entry into the world. Its mother gives birth standing up, so it falls about 6 feet to the ground. Mothers guard their calves from lions and other predators with powerful kicks. The newborn calf stands about 6 feet tall and weighs 200 pounds. Males will grow to 19 feet tall and up to 4,250 pounds. They live in the grasslands of Somalia, southern Ethiopia, and northern Kenya.

Grizzly bear cubs (usually twins) are born tiny in a midwinter den, but grow fast, up to 200 pounds their first year. The cubs remain with their mother, called a sow, for two to three years. Mother grizzlies are extremely protective of their cubs and teach them where to find roots, grasses, fruit, nuts, and other vegetation, which make up ninety percent of their diet. Bears also eat dead animals they find and occasionally they hunt. Grizzlies are now threatened but live in the uplands of western United States and Canada.

A female and male **gray wolf** raise a litter of five or six pups with the help of other adult wolves in a pack. The mother won't leave the den for the first few weeks after the pups are born, relying on the father to provide food for her. She and the pups then join the pack. A few weeks after being weaned, the pups join hunts to watch and learn, but won't actually hunt until they're about eight months old. Once endangered, their populations are now stable due to protection and reintroduction in wilderness areas of North America, Eurasia, and North Africa.

Guanaco females and their young live in small herds with only one dominant male. Every female has one calf, which is born ready to run within minutes. They live at high elevation throughout South America, grazing on vegetation. When a guanaco senses danger, it bleats a high-pitched call, alerting the herd to run swiftly, up to 35 miles per hour over steep, rocky terrain. Llamas, which have been bred to serve as pack animals, are the domesticated version of guanacos.

Female **white-tailed deer**, called does, give birth to one to three fawns each spring. Fawns wear a reddish-brown coat with white spots that helps them blend in with their surroundings. These spots fade by fall. They are also born without a scent so that predators can't easily smell them. A mother deer stays away from her fawn the first few days so that her scent doesn't rub off on it. White-tailed deer range throughout North America.

Giant pandas rarely give birth to more than one cub. Born nearly naked, pink, and blind, a cub weighs about 6 ounces and is one of the smallest baby mammals compared to its mother's size. Pandas are devoted mothers, caressing, cleaning, and holding their cubs constantly. Cubs stay with their mother for about two years. Due to deforestation and poaching, there are only about one thousand pandas left in the wild, living in bamboo forests on remote mountains in central China.

Musk oxen are more closely related to sheep and goats than to oxen. These shaggy animals are well adapted to life in the Arctic tundra. They can dig through snow with sharp hooves to graze on plants. Females, called cows, may not have calves after particularly harsh winters if food is scarce. Cows and calves bray to one another frequently within a herd. In addition to the circle guard formation, bulls will aggressively charge a predator with their sharp horns and massive bulk.

Baby **western harvest mice** are born naked and blind, but are weaned within three weeks. Litter sizes vary but can be up to twelve mice when food is plentiful. Females can have as many as fourteen litters every twelve months, which means one mouse may produce forty to eighty offspring a year! Mother mice weave their spherical nests in shrubs or on the ground throughout much of western North America.

An **American badger** gives birth to one to five cubs each March. The cubs stay in their mother's den for five to six weeks and strike out on their own by the end of summer. American badgers are found in central and western North America. They hunt small rodents by digging prey out of the ground with sharp claws.

Raccoons give birth to two to five kits each spring. A mother uses a tree hollow or rock crevice for her den. The kits are born blind and deaf but grow quickly and are ready to explore after three weeks. Raccoons are native to forests of North America. They are extremely intelligent and hunt birds, small mammals, crayfish, and fish. They also eat a wide variety of fruit and seeds.

An **eastern gray kangaroo** is a marsupial found in the forests of Eastern Australia and Tasmania. A newborn joey is born naked and blind and weighs less than a gram. After birth the tiny joey makes a monumental journey, crawling up its mother's hair till it reaches her pouch. There it nurses and grows for eleven months before it begins spending much time outside the pouch. It isn't fully weaned until eighteen months.

Virginia opossum (commonly called possum) are North America's only marsupial. A female often has more than a dozen babies in a litter, each baby so small that the entire litter could fit in a tablespoon. Babies spend the first few months in their mother's pouch, then later cling tightly to her back. Opossums scavenge for dead animals, garbage, and fruit, and hunt insects and small animals. When threatened they "play possum" by fainting and mimicking the appearance and smell of a dead animal. They range widely throughout Central America and much of the United States.

A female **plains zebra**, called a mare, gives birth to one foal every year. The foal has brown and white stripes that will turn to black and white as it gets older. Every zebra has its own unique pattern of stripes. The foal nurses on its mother's milk for up to a year. Able to stand and run within the first day of birth, foals join a herd of five to twenty zebras, living in the savanna grasslands of eastern and southern Africa.

The **hippopotamus** is semi-aquatic, inhabiting freshwater lakes and rivers in sub-Saharan Africa. Babies are born underwater and must swim to the surface to take their first breath. They often rest on their mother's back when in water and must swim underwater to suckle. Babies are fully weaned after a year. During the day, a hippopotamus stays cool in water or mud, then emerges at dusk to eat grass. They can weigh more than 4,000 pounds and are one of the most aggressive animals in the world.

Newborn **red fox** kits are blind and helpless. The mother, called a vixen, stays in the den with her pups for the first two to three weeks while the father, called a dog, brings food. After twelve weeks the kits are weaned and begin to accompany their parents on foraging trips. They learn to scavenge for dead animals, search for seeds and berries, and hunt small animals. Red fox are widespread across the Northern Hemisphere.

Meerkats are a small member of the mongoose family that live in the southern African plains. Living in elaborate underground burrows, they are swift hunters, eating mostly insects, small animals, and fruit. All members of the mob take turns caring for the pups, grooming and teaching them how to hunt and to be alert for danger.

Usually two to three **cougar** (also called puma or mountain lion) cubs are born to a mother, but sometimes up to six. Newborn cubs have spots that fade as they mature. A mother cougar is very protective and will even fight a grizzly bear to save her cubs. The youngsters stay with her for two years, learning to hunt anything from rodents to large game, mostly deer. Cougars have a wide range throughout much of North and South America.

A mother **chimpanzee** holds her infant constantly during its first five to six months of life. Later the youngster clings to her stomach and back. Young chimpanzees play, climb, and wrestle, and learn to build nests and groom one another. They also learn how to use tools like sticks to fish for termites. Females help one another with babysitting. The young aren't weaned until four to six years of age. They live in forested zones in west and central Africa.

African elephants are the largest land animals and have the longest pregnancy of any mammal—almost twenty-two months. At birth calves can weigh 200 pounds and take ten years or more to become full grown. Female elephants, called cows, live in family herds with sisters and grandmothers. The responsibility to protect calves falls to the entire family group. Adult males, called bulls, roam on their own. They live in central and southern Africa.

Ring-tailed lemurs are primates, related to monkeys and apes. Mothers usually have one or two babies. They live in social groups, called troops, with females caring for the young. Lemurs spend much of their time huddled together, keeping social bonds strong. They also like to sunbathe. Sitting upright with arms outstretched they face the sun and soak up warmth. Lemurs forage on fruit, leaves, flowers, tree bark, and sap. They are endangered, found only in Madagascar.

A mother **lion** usually gives birth to a litter of two to four cubs in a secluded den away from other lions. She protects and nurses them for six to eight weeks before bringing them into the pride. A pride consists of five to six related lionesses, their cubs, and one or two males. The females do most of the hunting, working together to bring down large game. Wild lion populations are currently declining but still exist in sub-Saharan Africa and Asia.

Mountain goats aren't true goats, but are properly known as goat-antelope. The females, called nannies, form nursery groups of up to twenty animals. Each spring a mother nanny gives birth to one kid, sometimes two. The kids are born to the high alpine mountains of western Canada and the United States. They are sure-footed from the start, running and climbing within hours of birth. But to be safe, their protective mothers often stand below them on steep slopes to stop any falls.

American pika give birth to two to four babies per litter. Babies are weaned at three weeks of age and grow to adult size within three months. They're very vocal, using warning calls to guard their territory and sound alarms for predators. Males use songs to attract females during mating season. Pikas live in boulder fields at high elevation in western North America. They survive the harsh winters by storing dried plants to eat later in piles called "haystacks" within their rocky dens.

One **sea otter** pup is born in water with a full coat of fur, which allows the pup to float. It begins to swim at four weeks but still spends most of its time resting on its mother's belly as she floats, or wrapped in kelp so it doesn't drift out to sea. Pups nurse for six to eight months while learning how to dive for food such as crabs, urchins, abalones, clams, and mussels. They are native to the coasts of the eastern and northern Pacific Ocean.

The name **orangutan** means "person of the forest." Only humans have a longer-lasting relationship than a mother orangutan with her infant. For the first two years the baby stays in constant contact with its mother, but it takes another eight years to become independent. Young orangutans are highly intelligent and must learn everything from their mothers, including how to use tools and how to build a shelter. They are in danger of becoming extinct in the wild and live only in Borneo and Sumatra.

Glossary

groom   In animals, the act of removing dirt and parasites from the fur, skin, and feathers of oneself or others. Often grooming is a social act within a close-knit group of animals.

litter   A group of baby animals delivered to one mother at one birth.

mammal   Any vertebrate (animal with a backbone) of the class Mammalia, usually characterized by a body more or less covered with hair, nourishing its young with milk from the mammary glands, and, with the exception of a few egg-laying animals, giving birth to live young.

marsupial   Opossums, kangaroos, wombats, and bandicoots. The females of most species have an external pouch within which the newborn offspring, born extremely underdeveloped, naked, and blind, are suckled and complete their development.

predator   A carnivorous (meat-eating) animal that exists by hunting other animals for food.

regurgitate   To surge or rush back undigested food from the stomach for feeding young animals.

suckle   To nurse (nourish) a baby animal with milk from the breast or udder.

wean   To adjust a young animal to food other than its mother's milk.

Sources

Elbroch, Mark & Kurt Rinehart. *Peterson Reference Guide to the Behavior of North American Mammals.* Boston: Houghton Mifflin Harcourt, 2011.

Kingdon, Jonathan. *The Kingdon Field Guide to African Mammals.* London: A & C Black Publishers Ltd., 2003.

Macdonald, David W. *The Princeton Encyclopedia of Mammals.* Princeton: Princeton University Press, 2009.

Menkhorst, Peter & Frank Knight. *Field Guide to Mammals of Australia.* New York: Oxford University Press, USA, 2011.

Nowak, Ronald M. *Walker's Mammals of the World.* Baltimore: The Johns Hopkins University Press, 1999.

Parker, Steve. *DK Eyewitness Books: Mammal.* New York: DK CHILDREN, 2004.

Reid, Fiona. *Peterson Field Guide to Mammals of North America: Fourth Edition.* Boston: Houghton Mifflin Harcourt, 2006.

Sterry, Paul. *Baby Animals, A Portrait of the Animal World.* New York: Smithmark, 2005.

Good Websites for Information on Animals

BBC Nature: bbc.co.uk/nature/wildlife
Enchanted Learning: enchantedlearning.com/subjects/animals/Animalbabies.shtml
National Geographic: animals.nationalgeographic.com/animals/
National Wildlife Federation: nwf.org/Wildlife.aspx
Ranger Rick: nwf.org/kids/ranger-rick.aspx
ZooBorns: zooborns.com/zooborns/

For Linda Pratt. Many thanks for your kind and gentle support.

ISBN 978-0-545-87430-4

12 11 10 9 8 7 6 5 4 3 2 1   15 16 17 18 19 20/0

Printed in the U.S.A.   08

First Scholastic printing, September 2015

Book design by Roberta Pressel